SPIRITUAL
ENERGY

POCKET EDITION

Published from
Mardukite Borsippa HQ, San Luis Valley, Colorado
Mardukite Academy & Systemology Society
for spiritual or educational purposes only

SPIRITUAL ENERGY

Systemology
Professional Course
Booklet #13

Developed by Joshua Free
for the Systemology Society

© 2023, JOSHUA FREE

ISBN : 978-1-961509-38-2

Pocket Paperback Edition — *December 2023*

mardukite.com

Chart Your Flight For Ascension...
Then Let Your Spirit Fly!

Unlock your ultimate spiritual potential by removing barriers to your true native state.

Learn how to easily attain Self-actualization and help to actualize others along the way.

A greater appreciation and understanding of *Spiritual Life* and *Existence* awaits you. Expand your reach to achieve your dreams.

Each 'Professional Course' lesson-booklet offers simple exercises and techniques that directly apply the philosophy of Systemology, assisting to increase your true knowingness, improve your capabilities in this life, and even decide what you will do in your next.

At the Mardukite Academy of Systemology, the 'Professional Course' lessons in this series are presented to Seeker's that have already completed the 'Basic Course', previously released as six lesson-booklets, or the six-in-one single volume edition "Fundamentals of Systemology."

This all new presentation of the Systemology 'Pathway-to-Ascension' takes Seekers and continuing students from "Zero" to "Infinity" at lightning-fast speeds!

Discover Who You Really Are...

Because You Were Never Human

Fundamentals of Systemology
Basic Course Lesson Booklet Series

The Pathway to Ascension
Professional Course Lesson Booklet Series

TABLET OF CONTENTS

PROFESSIONAL
COURSE
INTRODUCTION

WELCOME, SEEKER!
LET'S CHART YOUR JOURNEY ON THE PATHWAY

Systemology is a "holistic" approach to understanding the human experience. It is not actually a singular "subject" in itself, but rather, a new way in which to view the many subjects of *Life* and all *Existence.*

This is a professional course in *Systemology*—specifically, how to *apply* the spiritual philosophy of *Mardukite Systemology* as a personal *"Pathway" to Ascension.* Our *Systemology* is a new approach to *"Self-Actualization."* It is completely relevant for the modern age and the future; and quite different from any previous similar attempts, or other traditions, you might find. What's more: it is applicable to anyone with any background.

This *"Professional Course"* series of lessons (booklets) immediately follows the material given in the *"Basic Course"* series—available as six separate pocket-sized booklets, or in a single hardcover volume titled: *"Fundamentals of Systemology: A New Thought For The 21st Century."*

This is a *new* presentation of *Systemology*, emphasizing the application of our philosophy for those *Seekers* that are *"Flying-Solo"*—or else working through their studies and exercises as solitary practitioners. This is a new innovation for *Systemology*. Aside from the book *"Crystal Clear,"* all of our former advanced courses have placed a focus on *"Traditional Piloting"*—where experienced practitioners assist *Seekers* in *"processing."*

To receive the greatest benefit from this study: it is expected that a *Seeker* will already be familiar with the fundamental concepts and terminology (previously relayed in the *Basic Course*) before using lessons from the *Professional Course*. This will allow us to cover the extensive territory of the *Pathway* much more quickly. However, for reference, a basic "*glossary*" of vocabulary used in this lesson is provided in the "*appendix.*"

A NEW VIEW OF THE HUMAN SPIRIT

Systemology is not a religion and does not require any type of *faith*. It is, however, built upon a "spiritual" premise—and as such is an "applied spiritual philosophy." It is based on ancient teachings that we are *Spiritual Beings* essentially "wearing" bodies like clothes—or using them as "vehicles." Yet our true native nature is not *physical*, but beyond this existence; and we can certainly operate a "body" from *outside* of it.

We are **all** *Spiritual Beings*—each of us a *unit* of *Spiritual Awareness*—that have experienced a very long *Spiritual Timeline* of existence. Although we might be particularly attached to the familiar "physical shells" associated with *this* lifetime, our true *"Spiritual Lifetime"* is seemingly *eternal*. We have been many things before *Human*, and we go onward as a *Spiritual Being* after our *"genetic vehicle"* of *this* incarnation perishes.

While a "spiritual" view of the *Human Condition* may not seem unique to our philosophy, just how often is the concept treated *systematically*? For that matter: just how many people, supposedly raised to this or that religion, or professing to believe one thing or another, actually live their lives as though they are *Spirits*?

As *Spiritual Beings* of immortal existence and infinite potential, we are not simply the *"creations"* of an even greater *Being-*

ness; we are, in fact, an integral part of that *"creative force"* which permeates all existence.

Our basic nature is to be a *"creative being"*—our highest goals are *"to create."* And as such a being—which we refer to as an *Alpha-Spirit* in *Systemology*—we have run into some difficulties along the course of our *Spiritual Timeline* and found ourselves trapped within material *Universes* of our own collaborative *creation*.

Since we did not start out our existence in a trapped condition, it is correct to say that we have *"fallen"* from our native *"godlike"* states. It did not happen all at one, but progressively and systematically. We know our "troubles" have resulted from accumulated "barriers" and "blockages"—or *fragmentation*—during our vast experiences as *Spiritual Beings*. They are not because we lack something; but because of what's been added.

In *Systemology*, we systematically examine those routes by which we must have descended to reach our present condition, then reverse the direction of travel and chart a personal "*Pathway to Ascension*." Of course, the exact "details" of the *Spiritual Timeline* will be different for each individual *Seeker*. However, we have been able to systematically chart our *Pathway* based on common patterns of *Human fragmentation*.

In the most basic terms: the *fragmentation* that defines our "downward spiral" consists of decisions or considerations where we deny our true nature. This includes those decisions to "*withdraw*" rather than "*reach*"; where we choose to *not-know* rather than *know*; to *not-communicate* rather than *communicate*; and ultimately, to take *no-responsibility* for being a *creative-cause*, and therefore succumb to being an *effect*.

But there is *hope!* And much more importantly: there is an effectively workable *way out* of the mazes and traps of our existence. If you are reading this now, you have already begun to gather your tools and build up the *"horsepower"* necessary to break the gravity holding your *Spiritual Beingness* to the *Human Condition*.

STUDYING THE PROFESSIONAL COURSE

Most *Seekers* study and practice *Systemology* at-a-distance and independent of the "Mardukite Academy" or any "Master-level" mentors trained therein. This means that the *books* (and to a lesser degree, the *internet*) are the only means of direct contact a *Seeker* maintains with the "Systemology Society" during their studies. A continuing *Seeker* from the "*Basic Course*" will be familiar with the style of study found in *this* course.

Misunderstood words are the most common reason an individual abandons studying a subject. When a misunderstanding occurs, *Awareness* declines. These misunderstandings start to "stack up" after the first occurrence, and as a result, the level of interest and attention will also decline. This is how a "confusion" develops; and the individual will get "bored" with the subject, feel tired, and unable to concentrate.

One solution is to return to the part of the material that was still interesting and enjoyable to read. When scanning around that area of text, there is likely to be a new word (or new specific use of a familiar word) that is unclear, but was passed by unnoticed. All *Systemology* books include their own *glossary*. Using this *glossary* and a high-quality dictionary will help resolve this misunderstanding once it is located.

An effective education of any subject is taught on a *gradient*. This is what is intended by presenting the study of something as "*grades*." Rather than treating a subject as one total mass, true learning is achieved by increasing one's understanding with a *gradual* increase upward. The *ascent* to a mountaintop is not successfully achieved in one leap, but by targeting and reaching specific checkpoints along the way.

This *Professional Course* consists of a series of lessons (booklets) that gradually increase a *Seeker's* ability to understand and apply the practices and techniques of *Systemology* as a complete "*Pathway to Ascension*." It is an appropriate study for continuing *Seekers* (from the *Basic Course*), but also "advanced" *Systemologists*.

Each lesson (booklet) of the *Professional Course* applies *Systemology* to a particular subject (or focus). It is best if the entire course can be studied and applied in sequential order. These lessons also employ a style of practice or technique called "*Systematic Processing.*" An introduction to applying this methodology is provided in the final lesson (booklet) of the *Basic Course*—or in the "*Fundamentals of Systemology*" volume.

To study the *Professional Course* just like a student at the Academy: a *Seeker* reads through all instructional material and applies each exercise (or "*process*") presented in the text to the extent they comfortably can, before continuing on to the next lesson (booklet).

When first starting on the *Pathway* as a *Solo* practitioner, without the aid of an experienced *Pilot*, a *Seeker* shouldn't "push too hard" or allow themselves to get too "stuck" on any one area (lesson) or *process*. It is not expected that any one area will be completely handled when first introduced. For optimum results, it is expected that a serious *Seeker* will make more than one "pass" through the entire *Professional Course.*

The *Professional Course* is not altogether different from other forms of practical or technical education: where the instruction and exercises are delivered to a completion, and then a student further increases their abilities, strength and skill-level by applying additional practice throughout their life. Therefore, a student should not concern themselves with perfectly mastering each step (or lesson) before progressing forward.

Additional passes through the material are likely to result in different "*realizations*" (an increased *level of understanding*) than a previous time. New "layers" of *Knowingness* may now be accessible during a *process* that may not have been before. It is important to avoid invalidating the progress you've made just because one area is not completely handled right away, or if a certain *process* seems too difficult on the first pass.

CHARTING A COURSE ON THE PATHWAY

Although we can communicate a systematic structure to *fragmentation,* the personal journey experienced along the *Pathway* will be different for each *Seeker.* For example, certain areas will seem more "*turbulent*" or difficult for one *Seeker* than another. We tend to say that these areas have more "*charge*" on them—or that they are more "*heavily charged.*" It is best to handle such areas when you are already feeling "good" and not in a situation (or condition) where that specific area is consistently being "*triggered*" or "*restimulated.*"

As an applied philosophy, *Systemology* "theory" can be easily utilized in the "laboratory" of the "world-at-large" in everyday life. This is implied within the basic instruction of each lesson. Unlike other "sciences" that conduct experiments by making a change to some "objective variable" *out there* and waiting to see an effect, our focus is the individual (or *Observer*) themselves, and how *they* affect the "*Reality*" perceived.

In addition to applying *Systemology* "New Thought" to everyday life, our philosophy is applied by using specific exercises and systematic techniques. These "*processes*" provide the most stable personal gain (and *realizations*) for each area; but only when actually applied with a *Seeker's* full "*presence*" and *Awareness*.

This *Professional Course* is designed so that it may be easily read and studied with little concern for what "dangers" these teachings—or *processing*—might unleash. However, there are still some guidelines that pertain to the "best-uses" of these course lessons, particularly if a *Seeker* intends for stable development.

Skipping over too much material/*processing* in early lessons may make attempts to understand (or apply) later lessons more difficult. However, once the complete *Professional Course* is worked through at least once in its entirety, specific areas can then be later returned to and treated with a greater sense of *Awareness* and *"presence"* than before. Of course, in *"Traditional Piloting,"* the rate of processing is monitored by an experienced practitioner; but in *"Solo-Processing,"* a *Seeker* must regulate their own progress on the *Pathway.*

Applying a systematic technique is called *"running a process."* The *processes* are designed with very simple instructions or "command-lines." To run a processing command-line, a *Seeker* may be assisted by the communication of that *line* from a "Co-Pilot" (as in "Traditional Piloting"). But even then, a *Seeker* must still personally "input" the *command* as *Self*. For this reason —and quite thankfully—*Solo-Processing* is possible.

TAKING FLIGHT ON THE PATHWAY

Processing Techniques are intended to treat the *Spiritual Being* or *Alpha-Spirit*; the individual themselves. It is applied by the *Alpha-Spirit*—then *Self-directed* to the "Mind-System" or even a "body" (*genetic-vehicle*), both of which are "constructs" that the *Alpha-Spirit* (*Self*, or the "I-AM" *Awareness unit*) operates, but neither of which is actually *Self*. *Fragmentation* causes *Humans* to falsely identify *Self as* the "*Mind*" or even a "*Body*."

The *Professional Course* lessons (booklets) are designed for the *Beginning Seeker* in mind—one that may have an understanding of theory, but with little experience in practice. That being said: each of these lessons may be used toward total *Beta-Defragmentation* within a specific area. There are also more *processes* given for each subject than may be necessary to achieve an *ultimate end-point realization* on that entire area.

Some *processes* can be treated quite lightly at first; others may require a bit of working at in order to get *"running"* well. It is important to set aside a period of time when you can be dedicated to your studies and *processing*. This period of time is referred to as a *"processing session."* The reason for this, is that when a *process* does start *running* well, it is important to be able to complete it to a satisfactory *"end-point."*

The purpose of *systematic processing* is to be able to *really* "look" at things and even determine the *considerations* we have made—or attitudes we have decided—about *Reality* as a result of those experiences. It doesn't do us much good to simply "glance"—or to *restimulate* something uncomfortable and then quickly *withdraw* from it once again, leaving more of our *attention* yet again behind and held fixedly on it.

Generally speaking, a *Seeker* continues to *run* a *process* so long as something is "happening"—which is to say, the *process* is still producing a change. Usually this is evident by the type of "answers" that a *command-line* helps a *Seeker* originate from the database of their own *Mind-System*. The *command-lines* do not "do" anything on their own. They assist a *Seeker* to direct their own attention toward increasing *Awareness*.

Of course, a *Seeker* may also cease to generate new "data" from a *process* without reaching an *"ultimate" realization* as an *"end-point."* It is possible that additional "layers" (or even other "areas") require handling before anything "deeper" is accessible. If this is the case, end the *process*. But, if a *Seeker* is *withdrawing* from something uncomfortable that was incited or stirred up, then a *process* is *run* until they feel "good" about it.

In case the thought of encountering *"turbulence"* is a concern: the techniques given as *"Opening Procedures"* of a *Formal Session* (in the *Basic Course*), and those found in the earliest lessons of the *Professional Course*, are quite useful when applied as "safety nets" for maintaining *Awareness* and *presence*, even when *Flying-Solo*.

One of the benefits to *Flying-Solo* is that *processing* is entirely *Self-determined*. This already provides a certain built-in "safety" for a practitioner. Anything you *restimulate* by *Self-determinism* is *your thing*. It is not incited by external *other-determined* influences (or other "source-points" in existence) that make you an *effect*. It can be more easily handled in *processing*—or you can simply let things "cool down" and come back to it again.

While it may seem "mysterious" to beginners, a *Seeker* gets a sense for knowing how long to *run* a *process* only with practice. Once you have spent some time actually applying the *Professional Course*, there are many aspects that become "second nature" because they are, in fact, a part of our true original nature. All we have done is *"reverse engineer"* the routes of *creation* and *consideration* that are already *our own*.

LESSON THIRTEEN: SPIRITUAL ENERGY

INTRODUCING "ENERGY"

The remaining lessons of the *Professional Course* pertain to *Systemology Level-6*, which means that we are now treating areas officially considered *"Advanced Training"* or *"Ability Training."* Upper-levels are usually only introduced *after* a *Seeker* reaches a basic state of *"Beta-Defragmentation"* using previous processing-levels (*Systemology Level-0* to 5); and this requires a *Solo-Pilot* to make multiple passes through the material.

We introduce *Systemology Level-6* during the *Professional Course* to provide a greater sense of "completion" to the material we have covered—and to extend an invitation for *Seekers* to continue their progress with the *Advanced Ability Course* that will later follow (*scheduled for publication in 2024*). Upon reaching a basic state of *Beta-Defragmentation*, a *Seeker* is quite aware that there is much more of the *Pathway* ahead to still *reach* for; and they are quite ready and interested to *see what's next*. And our answer is: *Systemology Level-6*.

This lesson (booklet) introduces subjects that a *Seeker* may be familiar with—by label—from other *mystical* or *magical* materials and/or commonplace pop-culture representations of the "*New Age*." By this we mean other times "*Spiritual Energy*" is taught in terms of *chakras, auras, etheric bodies,* and the like. A *Seeker*/student is advised to study and practice these *metaphysical* areas *only within our Systemology* while on this course; and not presume to "know all about it," or mix previous interpretations with *this systematic methodology*.

Since the beginning of the *Pathway*, a *Seeker* is essentially dealing with "*energy*" in *systematic processing*. When we speak of *attention, circuits, flows, imprints* and *ment-*

al creations, we are actually treating *"energy"* indirectly. The entire *applied philosophy* of *Systemology* is in many ways entirely about *"energy"*—but we do not introduce any exercises aimed at directly *"handling energy"* until a *Seeker* has reached these *upper-levels.*

The *"spiritual weight"* of *fragmentation* entangled in the areas previously covered on this course is not all that *"holds us"* in *this Physical Universe (Beta-Existence). To* truly *"Ascend"* and be free of *this Beta-Existence is* to actually break the *"gravity"* or *"pull"* that this *reality* has on the *Awareness* of our *Beingness.* A *Seeker* will eventually have to be able to fully *confront, handle* and even *create "energy"* as an *Alpha-Spirit,* in order to reach the *"ultimate"* end of the *Pathway.*

The foundations of *this Beta-Existence* are based entirely on the use of *"force"* in order to maintain the level of *"solidity"* we experience *here* everyday. By *"force"* we mean *"energy* with *direction."* At the most physical level of its manifestation, we might equate this with *"effort."* But *Spiritual Energy*—or *"ZU"* (to revive a *6,000+* year old word for it)—is not limited only to expressions of *"effort"* demonstrated by *physical genetic-vehicles* or *bodies.* We are not restricted to only *handling energy* as it is expressed visibly in *this Universe* at all.

Beta-Existence is entirely composed of *energy;* but it is a type of *energy* that only operates in a *"space"* called: *"This Physical Universe."* An *Alpha-Spirit* that is convinced it *must rely* on *Beta-Existence* for its *energy* will never give up its own "hold on" it. There is a belief that all potential *energy-matter* of *all existences* is *"fixed"* (or *"conserved,"* as the standard physics theory is labeled)—limited to what is already provided for us, by some *other-determined source,* to *change* with *effort.* This falsehood is a large part of what keeps our *Awareness* of *Beingness* entrapped here.

Along the *track* of an individual's *spiritual descent* into the *reality-agreements* of *this Universe* and *Human Condition*, there is an incremental decline in the *Alpha-Spirit* maintaining itself as *"cause"* or *"source."* Rather than *cause* its own *effects* for-and-as *Self*, the *Being* decides on more and more "external" things to be *cause*, so that they may receive the *effects* of, for example, a *perception* or *sensation*. This establishes a very *real* (though *artificial* in *actuality*) "dependency" on the *Physical Universe* and *"Bodies"* in order to experience existence. It becomes practically a "spiritual addiction" that we typically can't shake off.

A complete mastery of *handling energy* exceeds the scope of this lesson. However, there are many *systematic processes* and exercises that help a *Seeker* develop more in specific areas, while at the same time

increasing their overall *"Actualized Awareness"* — the essential *"Spiritual Power"* that
the *Seeker* eventually must use to get free
of this *Beta-Existence.*

BASIC CHARACTERISTICS OF "ENERGY"

Seekers more easily understand the true
characteristics of *energy* after practicing
the procedures given for earlier *processing-levels.* This is because demonstra-
tions of *energetic characteristics* are
experienced during the *processes,* even
when they are not directly and distinctly
identified as such. Before getting too
deep into this area, we'll introduce the
idea of *"energy"* with light exercises you
can practice both indoors and outside.

A1. *"Spot an energy that could be helpful
     to you."*

A2. *"How could it be helpful?"*

B1. *"Spot an energy that could be helpful to others."*

B2. *"How could it be helpful?"*

A *Seeker* can *"Spot"* energies that are physically "visible" (such as a "light" that is "on"), or mentally *"Spot"* something apparent but hidden (such as the "current" in the walls feeding the "light"). There are no right or wrong answers here. It simply prepares a *Seeker* to *run* the following *process in-session*, listing as many *sources* as come up—whether *"Spotted"* as *real* in this *Beta-Existence*, or "conceptually" in another *Universe*.

1. *"Spot an energy source you find acceptable."*
2. *"Spot an energy source others would find acceptable.*

Control of a "system" consists primarily of the *start, stop*, or *change* of some *energetic-flow. Energy* simply *is* "energy." But when we *do* something *with* it, or *to* it, we are affecting its "*characteristics*" — or else making it the "type" of *energy* it is, or rather, how it is experienced.

A *Seeker* can physically practice *getting a sense* of *controlling* the "start" and "stop" of an *energy-flow* by, for example, using a functioning "light-switch" or simple "electronic device." Start with the switch in the "OFF" position. Alternate these *processing command-lines* ("PCL") a few times, or until you feel good about your actual perception of the *energy-flow*, even if only vaguely sensing it. [A similar *New Thought* exercise uses a "water-faucet" to practice *controlling* a "*flow.*"]

A. "*Mentally reach into the device (or circuit), permeate it, and perceive the 'no-flow' of energy.*"

B. "*Continue to mentally permeate it as you (physically) turn it on, and perceive the 'flow' of energy present.*"

Handling energy is not restricted to manifestations found in the *Physical Universe*. In the *"Magic Universe"* that precedes (or is a *level higher* than) *this Universe*, use of what *Humans* call the "electron" (as a *practical energy*), is *not* restricted to *flows* on "wired-circuits," or *consuming* a "limited resource" in order to *generate* it. There is still a use of focused *"energy,"* but by relative comparison to this *Beta-Existence*, experiences there really would seem much more *"magical."*

When a *Seeker* "mentally" handled *space* using *"dimension-points"* and *"corner-points"* (or *anchor-points*) in some exercises from earlier lessons, they were treating the most basic unit of *energy*. When *energy* is in *action* it takes on specific *characteristics*.

A *"flow"* is the characteristic of *energy* being *transferred* or *communicated*. For example: in *systematic processing*, we *run* "circuits" that represent specific *energy-flows*; such as an *"out-flow"* from you

41

to another "*terminal*" (lifeform, location, mass, *&tc.*), or an "*in-flow*" from a *terminal* to you. These are distinctions of the primary *flow-direction* of an *energy-beam*.

Direct practice with *energy-beams* is reserved for *upper-levels*, because if a *Seeker* starts working with them by trying to *do* something with them (to affect a visible change in *Beta-Existence*), the lack of response by the *Physical Universe* not only invalidates the *beam*, but also the *Seeker's* progressive development (*personal certainty*) for *creating energy-beams*. This also keeps many supposed "*magicians*" and "*mystics*" from ever achieving much actual experience in these areas.

The following mental exercise systematically practices *handling energy-beams* without attempting to overcome the *reality-agreements* of this *Physical Universe*. Even so, a *total certainty* or *mastery* is not expected in one sitting or *processing session* with the exercises in this lesson.

Many do not have a finite *end-point*, except a *Seeker's* own sense of improvement. Much like we might choose to regularly exercise to gradually build muscle for the physical *Body*, so too are there "spiritual muscles" that require incremental exercise regimens in order for us to regain *spiritual strength* and *ability*.

For this exercise, you *Imagine* (*visualize*) an *invisible energy-beam* hanging suspended in the air in front of you. An *energy-beam* is a sort of *free-standing wave*; it does not, itself, "emit" or "radiate" any *energy*. It also does not need to be "visible" to exist. These kinds of *beams* are used by an *Alpha-Spirit* to generate *motion*, or to "push" and "pull" at things—but that is not what we are doing in this exercise.

The first part of this practice simply requires *getting the sense* that there is an *energy-beam* there. Make it about three feet long, mentally viewed (*visualized*) as suspended in the air, unattached to anything that may be present in the environment.

Once the *idea* that *it is there* can be easily maintained (however "unreal" it may seem at first): repeatedly *alternate* "stretching" the *beam* out to six feet long, then back to three feet. For this exercise to be effective: it is important to not simply *"imagine/create"* the *beam* as suddenly two different sizes. First, you make a *"postulate"* or *"Alpha-Thought"* that it will *be* the size that it should be, and then you mentally "stretch" or "compress" the *beam* as part of the *visualization*.

Depending on how long the *process* is *run*, the *energy-beam* often has a tendency to "snap" or even resist being changed from one of the sizes. Regardless of what phenomenon is encountered, a *Seeker* just keeps working with it until the *energy-beam* is fully under their control—because after all, it *is their creation*. Although this practice seems trite or insignificant,

there is more to be gained here than may
be apparent at first sight.

HANDLING "ENERGY"

When first *processing* the *advanced-levels*
with *Traditional Piloting*, a *Seeker* is asked
to *"Look* over the *Body..."* (with eyes
closed, using *"ZU-Vision"*) and see if they
notice any *energy-beams* (or *flows*) that are
connected to it—or coming *in* to it *from*
some direction.

We don't simply occupy a "ring" of *360-
degree* perception, but instead, more of a
"sphere"—which means, we have at min-
imum, 129,600 (*360* multiplied by *360*)
points of potential "spiritual connectivity." Given the extent or duration of our
spiritual history (or *Backtrack*): no matter
which point or direction is randomly
chosen, there is likely to have been a *flow*
experienced from that direction.

Of course, this does not mean *every* one of these potential-points (or directions) must be *defragmented*, because an individual is not likely compulsively maintaining *all* of these *flows* in the *present*. It simply means that *any* one of them may be *run*. [The following instructions are adapted for *Solo-Processing*.]

Look over the *Body* (with eyes closed) and see if you get a sense for any *energy-beams* connected to it (from outside). These may only appear as very faint "threads"—or you may only get a vague sense of a *flow*. If you don't *see/sense* anything: simply *Imagine* (*visualize*) an *energy-beam* coming into the body briefly (without putting any *force* behind it) and then "*un-create*" it. Alternate this several times (*creating* and *un-creating*) and see if you get any impressions of *real energy-beams* coming into the *Body*; if not, leave this for a second pass through the course material.

Once you do get a *"real"* impression, it may be on *one* or *many* different *energy-beams* (from different directions). After you start handling them, it is quite possible that more will appear. Each *beam/flow* is either one *you* have *created* or *generated* at some point, or it belongs to someone else. While *running* this *process*, if it is not yours, it will detach and/or disappear; and if it is yours, it will turn a "golden" color when the *energy* is *defragmented* (or *"cleared,"* as some *New Age* practitioners say). Also, if it *is* yours, the *beam* may not entirely erase; but it should not seem "vivid" or "active" unless you specifically put your *attention* on it.

The entirety of this exercise consists of *Imagining* (*visualizing*) many *energy-beams* parallel (alongside) to any *beams* you found. It is preferable to use "golden" *beams* for this. If the new parallel *golden-beams* you are *visualizing/creating* start to "snap in" to the *"real"* one, then just keep "feeding" it many more of them until that stops happening—at which point it will *defragment* and/or *detach*. For now, simply clear up any *beams* that are obvious and easy to work with. In more *advanced-level* applications, you can eventually learn to "trace" the *source* of each active *energy-beam*, and find out who *created* it and what it's for (or connected to).

Fragmentation occurs because the *energy-flow* of our *attention* is *unknowingly*, *compulsively*, and *continuously* suspended on "things"—and we call *imprints* "things" because at low-*Awareness* levels, "thoughts" get *charged* with a lot of entangled *energy*, become a "*mass*" and seem quite "solid" as our *reality*. This is what results in "feeling depleted" as a *Being*—because *creation* only gives us things to *have*; it does not, by itself, actually provide us with *energy*.

In many ways, what is considered *energy* is an inversion (or opposite side) of what is considered *mass*. To be able to *handle energy*, one must also be able to handle (and *confront*) "*destruction*." Even on a "mental" or "spiritual" level, "*created energy*" is had by the *destruction* or "*dispersal*" of "*created mass*." Of course, the less an individual is able to handle *dispersal* of their own *creations*, the more "weighed down" they feel—and the less "*free attention-units*" they are able and willing to *Self-Direct*. "*Mass*" tends to restrict *free motion*.

Of course, to *create energy*, the *mass* must be *created* first; but since we have unlimited potential for *creation*, we also have an infinite supply of *energy*. Unlike what we are *implanted* to experience *as* the *Physical Universe*, our spiritual abilities require no esoteric "balancing act" regarding some fixed amount, or "conservation" (as the physicist says) of some "*energy-mass* equation."

Mental Imagery exercises from previous

lessons have mainly focused on *"creation"*—and our *processing* has been aimed at handling *"mass"* and *"terminals."* To *handle energy* as a *systematic process*, we have to go about it a little differently.

In actual practice, directly *Imagining (creating)* "energy"—or *mental images* of "energy"—is not an effective approach for *this* present level of *defragmentation* work and personal development.

In order to treat *energy*, we treat *destruction*. An individual must be able to handle *(confront)* both "creation" and "destruction" in order to regain *spiritual power*. "Power" comes as *both* combined— any *fragmentation* or reactive avoidance *(withdrawal)* with one, is to have inabilities with the other.

The *power* to *create* requires the *responsibility* and *control* of the same magnitude of *power* to *destroy*. And while we are really speaking of *spiritual abilities*, "thought-forms," and *Alpha* states, if a *Seeker* decides to take a "wider look," they may also see ways that this principle is demonstrated in the *Physical Universe* too.

As another matter of principle: we tend to *create* more than we "need" to be certain of our "*having*" things, or to maintain a certain satisfactory or acceptable condition of "*havingness*" (to be systematically accurate).

As a simple example: a farmer that needs *four* bushels of wheat to survive, plants *ten*. *Two* bushels worth get lost to some pestilence, *three* are sold to maintain other costs, and *one* is given to the *miller* to turn the other four into a usable grain-flour. These are not necessarily realistic quantities—the point is: more than *four* are planted. And we maintain similar *considerations* about our *creations*.

Now let us look more directly at how all

this applies to *Systemology* and why we cover some of these *advanced* areas in this *Professional Course*. There are a couple basic observations in physical science that ring true for all *Systems*.

When *energy* is condensed, it becomes *matter*; when *matter* is dispersed, it becomes *energy*.

A *dispersal*—such as an explosion—is really a *series* of energetic *"out-flows"* from a single (central) point.

These "facts" haven't changed.

The *"power"* a *Seeker* regains from *systematic defragmentation*, is not earned by simple "erasure" of *fragmentation* and *imprints*. We are actually "destroying" these *compulsive continuous creations*—but only *after* giving a *Seeker* the *certainty* that they can *create* any of them again at will. The entangled *energy* is restored "as *energy*" when the *mass* it once was (as an "*imprint*") is *destroyed*. A *Seeker* feels *"relief"* because their *persistent creation* (or *imprint*) is actually *"dispersed."* It doesn't just vanish or disappear; it *explodes.*

Therefore, at *Systemology Level-6*, instructions for *"mental imagery"* or *"handling energy"* involves a lot of *explosions.* And just *Imagining* "explosions" themselves is not effective for *processing.* The *ability-to-confront* "explosions" is critical for many reasons, but for present purposes, let us consider that: if you *Imagine* (*create/visualize*) a "rock" and then *"un-create"* by simply making it "disappear," there is no *energy gain.* If you, however, *decide* to *"blow it up,"* then you've just *created energy* from a formerly *created mass.*

There is no point in *destroying* our *finest creations*—all a *Seeker* needs to do to practice with this is to *Imagine* (*create*) tiny "particles" and make them "explode." Do this many times. Then practice making a *series* of small explosions along a line, as if burning up a piece of string. You can practice with eyes closed, then open. The purpose here is just to *get a sense* of the *energy* itself.

Once a *Seeker* has accomplished this and feels good about it on a smaller level: *Imagine* (*create*) incrementally larger objects (rocks, buildings, planets, galaxies) and have them explode. Also practice doing this on different sides (directions) of your *viewpoint*—such as "behind you" or "above you," &tc.

There are other basic manifestations of *energy* that include our perception of space. "Heat Energy" is millions of particles moving quickly, colliding and exploding. "Cold Energy" is millions of tiny "implosions" that actually slow and stop the motion of other particles. At this level of development: a *Seeker* may "play" with various "*mental exercises*" regarding *energy* and *explosions* freely.

Now let's consider some "*energy sources*"

as they exist in *Beta-Existence*. The most basic natural *energy source* that you are familiar with is the local *Sun* for which *this "Solar System"* of *planets* is named. One will notice that "THE SUN" is absent from our *tour of planets* in *Lesson-10*. We'll use it now for the next exercise.

A *Seeker* can refer back to earlier instructions for assistance—but the entirety of this exercise is to *get a sense* of being above the *Sun*, looking down at it; and then practicing some *reach* and *withdraw* (mentally connecting and letting go) until you get comfortable with its being there (which is the same as saying that you can comfortably *confront* its *existence*).

Once you are doing fine with being near the *presence* of the *Sun* (which, by the way, is quite different than the *presence* of a *planet*): *Spot* the motion and collision of particles within the *Sun* that is turning *destruction* into *energy*. Get a real sense of the *heat-energy* produced. Then continue

55

your mental *reach* and *withdrawal* with the *Sun* (while maintaining the *sense* or *Awareness* of the activity actually taking place within it).

Now *Imagine* (*create*) a "*copy*" of the *Sun* alongside it. *Spot* any differences between your *copy* and the *Sun*, and adjust your *visualization* by *intention*. When you're satisfied with your *copy*, make another *copy* on the other side of the original *Sun*. Continue to do this until you are comfortable with easily making *copies*.

To advance this further, if a *Seeker* is already well practiced with "*ZU-Vision*" or *spiritual perception*: *Spot* a different "*star*" —preferably one of a different color than the local *Sun*—and once there is a good perception of it, the above exercises are repeated on that "*star.*" Continue to do this with various *stars* until you are comfortable making *copies* of these as "*energy sources.*"

HANDLING "ENERGY-SYSTEMS"

After a *Seeker* is comfortable with the material and exercises in the previous section, the *Systemology* of *"personal energy-systems"* is introduced. In this area, our methods tend to overlap with various *mystical* teachings and practices that one might find in the *New Age*; but again, our treatment of it is *systematic*.

To *get a sense* of *"having energy"* or *"increasing energy"*: Imagine (*create*) many small *"sun-stars"* (a foot or so in size) in the *space* surrounding you, having them connect to you and "feeding" you *energy*. Continue to do this until you feel comfortable about *"having energy."* Then, make many even smaller *"sun-stars"* (an inch or so) all throughout the body, *getting a sense* that they are providing *heat-energy*. Do this for all the various parts of the body. [This is the true essence of anc-cient *"StarFire"* rituals that have since been confused with esoteric hype and blood rituals.]

Not surprisingly, one of the easiest ways of handling personal energy is also the most commonly known. For this, a *Seeker creates* and *in-flows* energy by *Imagining* a "cloud of golden energy" surrounding them, and "flowing it into" the *Body* intentionally using their *"breath."* Although this practice is commonplace, a *Seeker* should recognize that *they*—as an *Alpha-Spirit*—is *creating* this *energy-source;* that it is *not* coming from some obscure *other-determined external* "Divinity" or "Cosmic Source." [In spite of the language used by some *mystics*, if your goal is *Ascension*, there is no *"Cosmic Consciousness"* or *"Universal Mind"* present within *this Beta-Existence* that you are going to want to be "One" with.]

There is an entire spiritual philosophy behind *"breathing."* Most of it simply involves ways of delivering more oxygen to the body; or to regain *conscious control* of the automation associated with *"breathing."* Some of our earlier work in this area may be found in *"The Power of Zu"* volume of the *Systemology Core* (also published as *"Mardukite Zuism: Academy Lectures, Volume 5"*). But that is not essential to what we are dealing with here.

The *"in-flow with breath"* is used in *systematic processing* to "bypass" some of the *energy fields* and *spiritual machinery* that we have set up around us, which typically handles our *energetic* functions on an automatic basis (and which also includes a lot of defense mechanisms to prevent this kind of intentional tampering). [*Flowing-in* large *golden-clouds-of-energy* with *breath* does produce an effect; and it is for this reason that some *magical practitioners* have "stumbled on" sporadic results during varied eclectic *arcane* experiments.]

To do this effectively, a *Seeker* would practice what *mystics* refer to as "pore breathing"—where an individual *visualizes* the surrounding *golden energy* as completely permeating into the *Body* through all of its "pores" with each "breath." As a result, the *breathing* is generally slow and deliberate—but *attention* really doesn't need to be given to any particular "rhythm" or method otherwise.

This type of work leads us into our next area of handling *"personal energy-systems"* directly; and this is one of those subjects that a *Seeker* may have some familiarity with from other traditions and teachings. There is a lot of information available regarding what the *Eastern* practices refer to as the *"chakras"*—and it is by this label they are best known. The only concern in continuing to use the word *"chakra"* here, is if any of a *Seeker's* prior learning in this area inhibits their progress with our presentation of the *Pathway*; but if so, at this level of development, altering the label alone will probably not make much of a difference.

The *enlightened* among us have long understood that individuals in *this Universe* are *"microcosms"*—*"micro-cosmos," Universes* unto themselves—that reflect the same *Systemology* as what we treat as *Universes*.

In previous lessons, we described the *"condensation-of-universes"* that is mirrored in *kabbalistic* representations and other *esoteric* diagrams depicting various inter-dimensional *"levels"* or *"spheres."* By this we mean how *Universes* followed a certain sequence of "collapsing-in" on each other to bring us to *this* version of *Beta-Existence*.

Technically, our *considerations* for these "prior" *Universes* still *exist*; they have simply been "superimposed" upon several times since. The *energy* that went into the *foundations* of these *Universes* is still with us—but it is more *condensed* (there-fore more "*solid*") than what we experienced at "*higher-levels.*" But all of the *esoteric* associations—labeling various levels, color-coding them with "*mantras*" (intoned words) and notes of music—have not delivered anyone *out* of *this Universe.* Tables and charts do not substitute *Knowingness.*

The practices suggested are not particularly "difficult"—even reflecting some of what you might find dispensed from a basic newsstand "*How-To*" publication. Still, we do not introduce "*chakras*" officially to a *Seeker* until *after* they've completed *Beta-Defragmentation.* Getting a "*chakra-alignment*" or "*aura-cleanse*" is no stable substitute for the *Pathway.* In a state of *fragmentation,* any beneficial effects will have "peaked" within three days. Without *defragmentation,* the individual would be right back to where they were a week later. Such practices also tend to put the individual entirely at the *effect* end of another practitioner as *cause*.

PERSONAL ENERGY-SYSTEMS

In systematic terms: the *chakras* are *"meta-physical"* (*spiritual*) *energy-centers* that make up the *"personal energy-system"* that connects *"Bodies"* to *"Universes"* —anchors *"identities"* to *"existences."* Although there are hundreds of these *energy-centers*, we usually use the term *"chakras"* to refer to a specific central *"personal energy-system"* that consists of *seven-plus-one* (*eight*) of them operating as a network.

In our *Systemology*, the *"chakras"* directly align with what we have been working with—a "scale" of interaction (*communication*) between the *Alpha-Spirit* and *Beta-Existence*. This is why, at *Systemology Level-6*, a *Seeker* that is already familiar with our original *Standard Model*, the *Awareness Scale*, the *ZU-Line*, *Spheres of Existence*, and *Levels of Universes*, does not require any additional outside research or cultural-systems to compose (and understand) their own *"Master Chart"* of the *"chakras."* It is the same *seven-plus-one* (*eightfold*) *system* that we have been employing this whole time. That all being said, we give a *Seeker* some assistance in this area by synthesizing a new *Awareness Scale* for the *"chakras"* that summarizes the aspects of our philosophy (just listed above). Here we pair the data directly with *systematic correspondences* for the *"Standard Model."*

8. CREATION : "Infinity"

7. KNOWINGNESS : "Alpha Spirit"

6. PERCEPTION : "Alpha Thought"

5. COMMUNICATION : "Intention"

4. SYMBOLS : "The Mind System"

3. EMOTION : "Reactive Thought"

2. SEXUALITY : "Organic Sensation"

1. EATING : "Self-Survival"

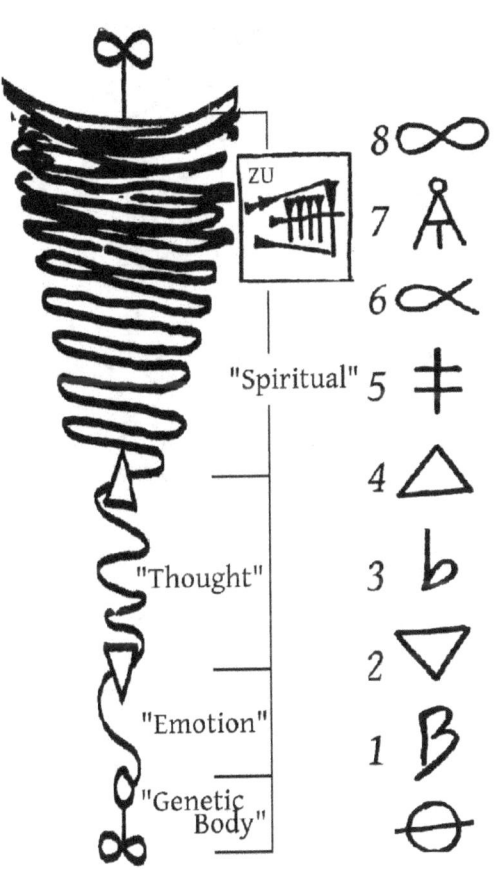

ZU

8 ∞

7 🜨

6 ∝

"Spiritual" 5 ‡

4 △

3 ♭

2 ▽

"Thought"

"Emotion"

1 ℬ

"Genetic
Body"

⊖

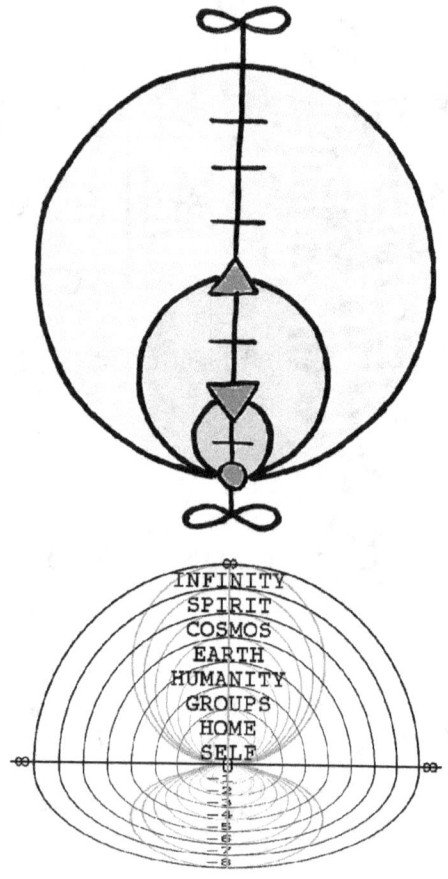

INFINITY
SPIRIT
COSMOS
EARTH
HUMANITY
GROUPS
HOME
SELF

And here we pair the new *Awareness Scale* with our *"Spheres of Beta-Existence"* data.

8. CREATION : "Infinity"
7. KNOWINGNESS : "Spirit"
6. PERCEPTION : "Cosmos"
5. COMMUNICATION : "Earth/Life"
4. SYMBOLS : "Humanity"
3. EMOTION : "Groups"
2. SEXUALITY : "Home/Family"
1. EATING : "Self"

It is also important to note that this *"personal energy-system"* runs parallel with previous *"Universes"* where we have experienced being *"identified with a body."* These *"chakras"* are still carried with us from our former occupations of *Bodies* that we consider relatively *"more subtle"* in their *solidity.* As long as we have been "using" *Bodies,* we have maintained a *"personal energy-system"* in which to *anchor* them in a *Universe.* The *Systems* for former *Bodies* are "collapsed/condensed" and carried forth by an *Alpha-Spirit* into *this Universe.*

For example: the "survival" emphasis of *this Game-Universe* is based on "preservation of a *Body*" as the most fundamental goal. This follows well with keeping people in conflict for superiority and domination. The underlying principle connecting these two factors is *"To Eat"* (and to a lesser extent, *To Consume*). This is the lowest possible common denominator (or factor) of the currently existing sequence of *Universes*—of which the other *"higher"* ones have since *"collapsed-in"* to. As such, it is directly linked to the *lowest* "root" *chakra*, that is aptly named because it is literally what *roots* or *anchors* us exclusively to *this Beta-Existence*.

We have every reason to believe that prior to the *condensation* of *this Beta-Existence*, the "personal energy-system" used in the prior *"Magic Universe"* was linked to a slightly less "solid" *Body*, and *"rooted"* to *that Universe* with what we would now consider the *"second lowest chakra."* This

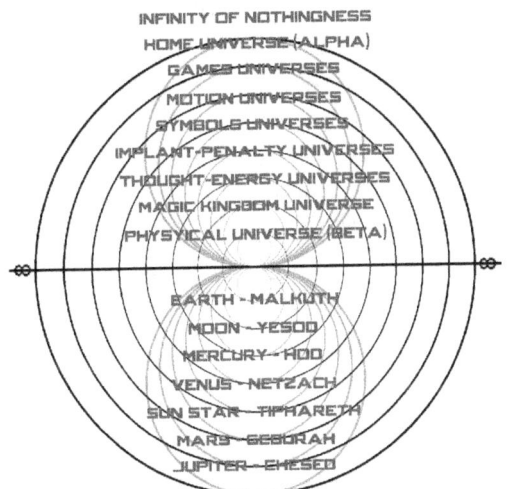

INFINITY OF NOTHINGNESS
HOME UNIVERSE (ALPHA)
GAMES UNIVERSES
MOTION UNIVERSES
SYMBOLS UNIVERSES
IMPLANT-PENALTY UNIVERSES
THOUGHT-ENERGY UNIVERSES
MAGIC KINGDOM UNIVERSE
PHYSICAL UNIVERSE (BETA)

EARTH – MALKUTH
MOON – YESOD
MERCURY – HOD
VENUS – NETZACH
SUN STAR – TIPHARETH
MARS – GEBURAH
JUPITER – CHESED

would make sense since the underlying "*game-goals*" of the *Magic Universe* focused much more on hedonistic pleasure: "*To Enjoy.*" At our present level of existence, this would be primarily equated to sexual sensation and intimacy.

In systematically describing *the Physical Universe* and the *Magic Universe* in this way, we have also explained the function

(or *"energetic domains"*) of the *lowest* ("1")
and *second-lowest* ("2") of the *"chakras."* It
may help to envision the *"root chakra"* as
in the vicinity of the feet, "grounding"
one's *Body* to the *Earth* (though most interpretations assign it to the region of the
"rectum"). The *second chakra* is tradition-
ally nearest the genitals or sexual organs
(with obvious connections to that depart-
ment). In regards to *Universes,* these are
the two we have the most data for.

The *third chakra* ("3") is located near the
stomach. It primarily governs emotions
and emotional responses. In relation to
the *"spheres,"* it concerns *"group energy"* —
or *"synergy"* —which is highly energetic
and emotional in content, though not necessarily as intimate as what is handled
with the *second chakra.*

The *fourth chakra* ("4") is also known as
the *"heart chakra"* because of its location
and association with compassion. However, on a systematic level, it essentially

governs *energy* associated with *"signific-ances"* and *"importance"*—which at the general *societal* (or *Human*) level of inter-action, is represented by "broad symbols" rather than "specific" things.

The *fifth chakra* ("5") concerns our interac-tions or *communication* with other living beings. It is located near the throat and is often associated with "speech." It is dis-tinctly connected to the *"sphere of living-ness"* (or *All Life on Earth*), since living things are in communication with one an-other much differently than how we are in contact with the inert matter of the *Universe*.

The *sixth chakra* ("6") is usually near the eyes, from which we consider our ability to *"look"*—or else *"perceive"*—that there is a "world" or *Beta-Existence* "out there" in which to interact with. In terms of our *Standard Model*, this is the original "level" of *Awareness* at which an *Alpha-Spirit* first "entered-in" to *Shared/Games Universes*;

71

thus it concerns an ability to *perceive* things apart from our own *creations* and total *Knowingness*. Systematically, this is the point when we first permitted ourselves to *"Not-Know,"* so that we would have something to *"perceive"* or *"know about."*

The *seventh chakra* ("7") is often referred to as the *"third eye"* (located near the region of the forehead, above the eyes). On all of our models and scales, we typically associate this level with the *Alpha-Spirit* itself, as a *Spiritual Awareness*. But, for practical purposes, this is the same as referring to our original native state of *Total Knowingness*. In terms of *Beta-Existence*, it provides that "intuitive" degree of *Knowingness* of what we would otherwise have to *"look for"* or *"find out about"*—and which often defies *"reason."* [In a *fragmented* state, what usually passes for "human intuition" is really *reactivity* and *imprinting*; not this upper-level of true *Knowingness*.]

Finally, the *highest chakra* ("8") is essentially the *"godhood chakra"*—and we always systematically represent the *"highest"* ideal or aspect as the *eighth* (or with an "8") to demonstrate its *Infinity*. Nothing is *higher* than (or *beyond*) *"Infinity"*; and *"Nothingness"* is *"Infinity"*—but within that state is the "absolute potential" for the *creation* of *"Everythingness"* (as reflected by the actual manifestation existing throughout *lower levels of creation*). At the *highest* level, there is only the *pure Awareness* of "I-AM."

DEFRAGMENTING "ENERGY-SYSTEMS"

The *chakras* are obviously not "physical constructs" that are a part of the "physical anatomy" of the *Body*. The idea that they are "located within" is more figurative or conceptual. They track along, parallel, to the *Body* that we *identify* with as

73

"ours"—but operate at a higher-degree of "spatial" existence. They also correlate with the other "astral" layers or "auric" body-like *fields*, which we still carry with us from these *higher*/former *Universe* experiences—and which *mystics* and *spiritualists* have been aware of for a long time.

The word "chakra" is *Sanskrit* and implies a "spinning disc" or *wheel*. Although we tend to conceptualize them as "balls" or "globes," that is only how they *appear*. The "disc" is simply spinning so fast that it appears quite "sphere-like" (like when you "spin a coin" on a table-surface). They are also quite "reflective"—much like the *discs* used for music and video medias today. This gives them a quite radiant "metallic" appearance with a slight "sunburst" quality.

To begin systematically working with (and *defragmenting* or *clearing*) *chakras* as *energy-centers*, it is important for us to get an *actual* sense for where they are "functioning" relative to the *Body*. Although our emphasis is on the *chakras*, we start with a general *"ZU-Vision"* technique for locating something by increasing spiritual perception. Instead of explaining a lot of theory behind the exercise, let's just get right into it.

The technique simply requires *visualizing* "approximations" of a *thing* in various places until it starts to "feel right"—or rather, the *visualization* starts to get "pulled into" its correct shape and location. In brief: this operates on a systematic theory that as your *ability* to *create* a "thing" increases, so does your level of *perception* and *Knowingness* (about that *thing*). We use an "approximation" because this technique is more effective the "closer" you already are to what you're treating. In this case, we're handling *chakras.*

For applying this to *chakras*: Imagine (*visu-*

alize/create) *"spinning discs"* of *energy* around the *Body*. For this, we *don't* start by making them *in* the *Body*, so that we are not in *conflict* with *actual energies*. So we start with a bit of "testing" to try and *perceive* what *is* there rather than fight with it or force anything with our *visualizations*. You just keep placing these *"spinning discs"* of *energy* on all sides around you, above and below. As you keep doing this, you may *get a sense* that they should look or be a certain way; in which case, you go ahead and start making them that way.

After a *Seeker* has done this for a while—given that the *"intention"* and *"attention"* has been on *locating* and *perceiving* the *chakras*—the created *"spinning discs"* should develop a tendency to get "pulled in" to the *Body* (or possibly "snapping in") at their appropriate locations. Rather than change what you're doing, just keep "feeding" the *Body* these *"spinning discs"* by continuing to put them around the *Body* and allowing them to naturally get "drawn in." Eventually, *perception* on the *actual chakras* should gradually increase. A *Seeker* applies "*ZU-Vision*" primarily for this, with eyes closed, adjusting their *spirit vision* (by *intention*) to the "frequency-band" or *level* of the *chakras* while *looking* at the *Body*. This exercise is practiced until a *Seeker* is satisfied with their ability to *perceive* the *chakras*.

Now there is the matter of *defragmenting/clearing* the *chakras*, which itself requires some explanation. The *chakras* are essentially parts of a "*personal energy-system*," but it is not a "closed-system." These *spinning discs* or *wheels* are just one part of the "*spiritual machinery*" we maintain a *creation* of *unknowingly*. While we experience *Beta-Existence* at its "normative" *Human* range of sensory-*Awareness*, the *chakras* also automatically "cycle" or "process" the actual *spiritual energy-flows* that we are interacting with. Of course, each *chakra* tends to filter its own specific "area/level" or "domain" as we've described by numbering them.

Spiritual "health"—such as the "condition" of the *chakras*—is closely integrated with the general state of *fragmentation* or *Self-Honesty* that an individual maintains or experiences. This means that a lot of what a person hopes to "fix" with *chakra-clearings* or *aura-cleanses* is really handled with *defragmentation processing* in our tradition or philosophy. In our opinion, our methods provide more stable long-lasting results by correcting how an individual is *operating*, rather than spending all one's *attention* on constantly *cleaning up*.

The *chakras* each have the basic characteristics (or domains) as described in the previous section. These are simply areas of potential *fragmentation*. Some *mystics* describe various "overactive" and "underactive" qualities—but it really all adds up to *fragmentation* connected to each of those domains. For example: issues with physical illness pertain to the *first chakra*; relationship problems or perversions primarily denote *fragmentation* of the *second chakra*; and so on. Therefore we can also list "opposite" characteristics of an *inverted-Awareness Scale*, each demonstrating the extreme *antithesis* of a specific domain.

(+8) Creation; (–8) Destruction
(+7) Knowingness; (–7) Mystery
(+6) Perception; (–6) Delusion
(+5) Communication; (–5) Isolation
(+4) Symbols; (–4) Barriers/Enslavement
(+3) Emotion; (–3) Misemotion/Hate
(+2) Sexuality; (–2) Perversion
(+1) Eating; (–1) Physical Illness

The present author spent *thirty years* pursuing esoteric mysteries and arcane teachings. While the actual existence of these *energy-centers* is well observed throughout many traditions and many labels, it has become clear that there is no consistency between various interpretations of the "colors" or "geometry" of the *chakras*. As far as can be determined, their structure is likely to be *perceived* differently by different practitioners. In our tradition, we apply methods that were developed for *20th Century American New Thought*; and these may differ from what you may have learned from other "*New Age*" sources.

For example: we treat all of the *chakras* as a "*golden*" color, but with a faint prismatic rainbow effect as the *disc spins*—like what you see on a *compact-disc* or *DVD* surface when you angle it in the light a certain way. This also makes it easier to treat them all with the same style of technique that we've already been using.

The type of *fragmentation* that "*spiritual energy clearing practitioners*" describe will usually appear like black spots or dark discolorations. This is the "*energy-mass*" of *fragmentation* that is restricting an otherwise *clear channel* of the appropriate energy for that *chakra*. We handle this in *Systemology Level-6* to mainly "clean up" residual effects, because we have been indirectly *defragmenting* the *chakra* "domains" all along the *Pathway*.

While you can technically apply some *attention* toward a "dark area" and get it to turn white by *intending* or *creating* a small stream of neutral or golden energy into it, this does not solve what *caused* the misalignment in the first place.

Introducing these methods too early might just make an individual *more comfortable* with their *fragmentation* rather than handle it. *Defragmentation* only comes about from actually *confronting* something with *Awareness*; certainly not by *withdrawing* and pretending things aren't there.

We will end this lesson with a *systematic*

processing technique for *defragmenting* the *chakras*, based on the descriptions provided to a *Seeker* previously in this lesson. This should also only be handled *after* a *Seeker* is comfortable with the other exercises given previously in this lesson.

A. *"Close your eyes; alternately spot three points in the chakra, and three points in the room."*

B1. *"Spot things in the Universe that the chakra might be connected to."*

B2. *"For each thing: alternately spot the chakra and the connection to it."*

C1. *"Look for areas causing 'dark spots', or turbulence in the energy-flow, and spot what they are connected to."*

C2. [*Handle the fragmented area directly with one of the processes in the Professional Course; or simply handle it as a 'protest' as given in the next steps. See also: Lesson-4.*]

D1. *"Spot what is being 'protested' in connection with the area."*

D2. *"Alternate 'protesting' and 'admiring' it, until the energy begins to flow freely again."*

The general guidelines (about *chakras*) provided within this lesson are the most common workable factors that a *Seeker* may incorporate, and have actual certainty on, at *Systemology Level-6*. There is obviously more to each of the areas our *Professional Course* covers, but we have focused on making a concise consolidation of the most critical points necessary to compose a complete and workable *paradigm* or *applied philosophy*.

The Systemology Professional Course
continues in the next lesson booklet:
SPIRITUAL MACHINERY

GLOSSARY

actualization : to make actual, not just potential; to bring into full solid Reality; to realize fully in *Awareness* as a "thing."

agreement (reality) : unanimity of opinion of what is "thought" to be known; an accepted arrangement of how things are; things we consider as "real" or as an "is" of "reality"; a consensus of what is real as made by standard-issue (common) participants; what an individual contributes to or accepts as "real"; in *Systemology*, a synonym for "*reality.*"

alpha : the first, primary, basic, superior or beginning of some form; in *Systemology*, referring to the state of existence operating on spiritual archetypes and postulates, will and intention "exterior" to the low-level condensation and solidarity of energy and matter as the 'physical universe' (*beta*).

alpha-spirit : a "spiritual" *Life*-form; the "true" *Self* or I-AM; the *individual*; the spiritual (*alpha*) *Self* that is animating the (*beta*) physical body or "*genetic vehicle*" using a continuous *Lifeline* of spiritual ("*ZU*") energy; an individual spiritual (*alpha*) entity possessing no physical

85

mass or measurable waveform (motion) in the Physical Universe as itself, so it animates the (*beta*) physical body or "*genetic vehicle*" as a catalyst to experience *Self*-determined causality in effect within the *Physical Universe*; a singular unit or point of *Spiritual Awareness* that is *Aware* that it is *Aware*.

alpha thought : the highest spiritual *Self-determination* over creation and existence exercised by an Alpha-Spirit; the Alpha range of pure *Creative Ability* based on direct postulates and considerations of *Beingness*; spiritual qualities comparable to "thought" but originating in Alpha-existence, independently superior to a Mind-System.

ascension : actualized *Awareness* elevated to the point of true "spiritual existence" exterior to *beta existence*. An "Ascended Master" is one who has returned to an incarnation on Earth as an inherently *Enlightened One*, demonstrable in their words and actions; they have the ability to *Self-direct* the "Mind" and "Body" as *Self* (as a "Spirit"); and to maintain consciousness as a personal identity continuum with the same *Self-directed* control and communication of Will-Intention that is exercised, actualized and developed deliberately during one's present incarnation.

associative knowledge : significance or meaning of a facet or aspect assigned to (or considered to have) a direct relationship with another facet; to connect or relate ideas or facets of existence with one another; in traditional systems logic, an equivalency of significance or meaning between facets or sets that are grouped together, such as in *(a + b) + c = a + (b + c)*; in Systemology, erroneous associative knowledge is assignment of the same value to all facets or parts considered as related (even when they are not actually so), such as in *a = a, b = a, c = a* and so forth without distinction.

attention : active use of *Awareness* toward a specific aspect or thing; the act of "attending" with the presence of *Self*; a direction of focus or concentration of *Awareness* along a particular channel or conduit or toward a particular terminal node or communication termination point; the Self-directed concentration of personal energy as a combination of observation, thought-waves and consideration; focused application of *Self-Directed Awareness*.

awareness : the highest sense of-and-as *Self* in knowing and being as I-AM (the *Alpha-Spirit*); the extent of beingness directed as a viewpoint (POV) experienced by *Self* as *Knowingness*.

beta (awareness) : all consciousness activity ("*Awareness*") in the "Physical Universe" (KI, in *Zuism*) or else in *beta-existence*; *Awareness* within the range of the *genetic-body*, including material thoughts, emotional responses and physical motors; personal *Awareness* of physical energy and physical matter moving through physical space and experienced as "time"; the *Awareness* held by *Self* that is restricted to an organic *Lifeform* or "*genetic vehicle*" in which it experiences causality in *beta-existence*.

beta (existence) : all manifestation in the "Physical Universe" (KI, in *Zuism*); the conditions of *Awareness* for the *Alpha-spirit* (*Self*) as a physical organic *Lifeform* or "*genetic vehicle*" in which it experiences causality in the *Physical Universe*.

charge : to fill or furnish with a quality; to supply with energy; to lay a command upon; in *Systemology*—to imbue with intention; to overspread with emotion; personal energy stores and significances entwined as fragmentation in mental images, reactive-response encoding and intellectual (and/or) programmed beliefs.

channel : a specific stream, course, current, direction or route; to form or cut a groove or ridge or otherwise guide along a specific course; a direct path; an artificial aqueduct created to connect two water bodies or water or make travel possible.

circuit : a circular path or loop; a closed-path within a system that allows a flow; a pattern or action or wave movement that follows a specific route or potential path only; in *Systemology*, "*communication processing*" pertaining to a specific *flow* of energy or information along a channel; "*feedback loop.*"

communication : successful transmission of information, data, energy (&tc.) along a message line, with a reception of feedback; an energetic flow of intention to cause an effect (or duplication) at a distance; the personal energy moved or acted upon by will or else 'selective directed attention'; the 'messenger action' used to transmit and receive energy across a medium; also relay of energy, a message or signal—or even locating a personal POV (viewpoint) for the Self—along the *ZU-line*.

condense (condensation) : the transition of vapor to liquid; denoting a change in state to a more substantial or solid condition; leading to a more compact or solid form.

confront : to come around in front of; to be in the presence of; to stand in front of, or in the face of; to meet "face-to-face" or "face-up-to"; additionally, in *Systemology*, to fully tolerate or acceptably withstand an encounter with a particular manifestation without an automatic reactive response.

consideration : careful analytical reflection of all aspects; deliberation; determining the significance of a "thing" in relation to similarity or dissimilarity to other "things"; evaluation of facts and importance of certain facts; thorough examination of all aspects related to, or important for, making a decision; the analysis of consequences and estimation of significance when making decisions; also in *Systemology*, the *postulate* or *Alpha-Thought* that defines the state of *beingness* for what something "*is.*"

defragmentation : the *reparation* of wholeness; collecting all dispersed parts to reform an original whole; a process of removing "*fragmentation*" in data or knowledge to provide a clear understanding; applying techniques and processes that promote a *holistic* interconnected *alpha* state, favoring observational *Awareness* of continuity in all spiritual and physical systems; in *Systemology*, a "*Seeker*" achieving actualized "*Self-Honest Awareness*" is said to be in a basic state of *beta-defragmentation*, whereas *Alpha-defragmentation* is the rehabilitation of the *creative ability*, managing the *Spiritual Timeline* and the POV of *Self* as Alpha-Spirit (I-AM).

existence : the *state* or fact of *apparent manifestation*; the resulting combination of the Principles of Manifestation: consciousness, motion and substance; continued *survival*; that which independently exists.

exterior : outside of; on the outside; in *Systemology*, we mean specifically the POV of *Self* that is *'outside of'* the *Human Condition,* free of the physical and mental trappings of the Physical Universe; a metahuman range of consideration; see also *'Zu-Vision'*.

external : a force coming from outside; information received from outside sources; in *Systemology*, the objective *'Physical Universe'* existence, or *beta-existence*, that the Physical Body or *genetic vehicle* is essentially *anchored* to for its considerations of locational space-time as a dimension or POV.

fragmentation : breaking into parts and scattering the pieces; the *fractioning* of wholeness or the *fracture* of a holistic interconnected *alpha* state, favoring observational *Awareness* of perceived connectivity between parts; *discontinuity*; separation of a totality into parts; in *Systemology*, a person outside of *Self-Honesty* is said to be operating from a *fragmented* state.

flow : movement across (or through) a channel (or conduit); a direction of active energetic motion, typically distinguished as either an *in-flow*, *out-flow* or *cross-flow*.

genetic-vehicle : a physical *Life*-form; the physical (*beta*) body that is animated/controlled by the (*Alpha*) *Spirit* using a continuous *Spiritual Lifeline* (ZU); a physical (*beta*) organic receptacle and catalyst for the (*Alpha*) *Self* to operate "causes" and experience "effects" within the *Physical Universe*.

harmful-act : a counter-survival mode of behavior or action (esp. that causes harm to one of more *Spheres of Existence*)—or—an overtly aggressive (hostile and/or destructive) action against an individual or any other *Sphere of Existence*; in *Utilitarian Systemology*—a short-sighted (serves fewest/lowest *Spheres of Existence*) intentional overtly harmful action to resolve a perceived problem; a revision of the rule for standard *Utilitarianism* for Systemology to distinguish actions which provide the least benefit to the least number of *Spheres of Existence*, or else the greatest harm to the greatest number of *Spheres of Existence*; in *moral philosophy*—an action which can be experienced by few and/or which one would not be willing to experience for themselves (*theft, slander, rape, &tc*); an iniquity or iniquitous act.

hold-back : withheld communications (esp. actions) such as "*Hold-Outs*"; intentional (or automatic) withdrawal (as opposed to reach); Self-restraint (which may eventually be enforced or automated); not reaching, acting or expressing, when one should be; an ability that is now restrained (on automatic) due to inability to withhold it on Self-determinism alone.

hold-outs : in photography, the numerous snapshots/pictures withheld from the final display or professional presentation of the event; withheld communications; in Utilitarian Systemology— energetic withdrawal and communication breaks with a "*terminal*" and its *Sphere of Existence* as a result of a "*Harmful-Act*"; unspoken or undiscovered (hidden, covert) actions that an individual withholds communications of, fearing punishment or endangerment of *Self-preservation* (*First Sphere*); the act of hiding (or keeping hidden) the truth of a "*Harmful-Act*"; a refusal to communicate with a *Pilot*; also "*Hold-Back.*"

holistic : the examination of interconnected systems as encompassing something greater than the *sum* of their "parts."

Human Condition : a standard default state of Human experience that is generally accepted to be the extent of its potential identity (*beingness*) —currently treated as *Homo Sapiens Sapiens,* but which is scheduled for replacement by *Homo Novus* (the "New Human").

imagination : ability to create *mental imagery* in one's Personal Universe at will and change or alter it as desired; the ability to create, change and dissolve mental images on command or as an act of will; to create a mental image or have associated imagery displayed (or "conjured") in the mind that may or may not be treated as real (or memory recall) and may or may not accurately duplicate objective reality; to employ *creative abilities* of the Spirit that are independent of reality agreements with beta-existence.

imprint : to strongly impress, stamp, mark (or outline) onto a softer 'impressible' substance; to mark with pressure onto a surface; in *Systemology*, used to indicate permanent Reality impressions marked by frequencies, energies or interactions experienced during periods of emotional distress, pain, unconsciousness, loss, enforcement, or something antagonistic to physical (personal) survival, all of which are are stored with other reactive response-mechanisms at lower-levels of *Awareness* as opposed to the active memory database and proactive processing center of the Mind; an experiential "memory-set" that may later resurface—be triggered or stimulated artificially—as Reality, of which similar responses will be engaged automatically; holographic-like imagery "stamped" onto consciousness as composed of energetic *facets* tied to the "snap-shot" of an experience.

imprinting incident : the first or original event

instance communicated and *emotionally encoded* onto an individual's "*Spiritual Timeline*" (recorded memory from all lifetimes), which formed a permanent impression that is later used to mechanistically treat future contact on that channel; the first or original occurrence of some particular *facet* or mental image related to a certain type of *encoded response*, such as pain and discomfort, losses and victimization, and even the acts that we have taken against others along the *Spiritual Timeline* of our existence that caused them to also be *Imprinted*.

intention : directed application of Will; to intend (have "in Mind") or signify (give "significance" to) for or toward a particular purpose; in *Systemology* (from the *Standard Model*)—the spiritual activity at WILL (5.0) directed by an *Alpha Spirit* (7.0); the application of WILL as "Cause" from a higher order of Alpha Thought and consideration (6.0).

interior : inside of; on the inside; in *Systemology*, we mean specifically the POV of *Self* that is fixed to the '*internal*' Human Condition, including the *Reactive Control Center* (RCC) and Mind-System or *Master Control Center* (MCC); within *beta-existence*.

internal : a force coming from inside; information received from inside sources; in *Systemology*, the objective experience of *beta-existence* associated with the Physical Body or *genetic vehicle* and its POV regarding sensation and perception; from inside the body; in the body.

invalidate : decrease the level or degree or *agreement* as Reality.

mental image : a subjectively experienced "picture" created and imagined into being by the Alpha-Spirit (or at lower levels, one of its automated mechanisms) that includes all perceptible *facets* of totally immersive scene, which may be forms originated by an individual, or a "facsimile-copy" ("snap-shot") of something seen or encountered; a duplication of wave-forms in one's Personal Universe as a "picture" that mirror an "external" Universe experience, such as an *Imprint*.

perception : internalized processing of data received by the *senses*; to become *Aware of* via the senses.

pilot : a professional steersman responsible for healthy functional operation of a ship toward a specific destination; in *Systemology*, an intensive trained individual qualified to specially apply *Systemology Processing* to assist other *Seekers* on the *Pathway*.

point-of-view (POV) : a point to view from; an opinion or attitude as expressed from a specific identity-phase; a specific standpoint or vantage-point; a definitive manner of consideration specific to an individual phase or identity; a place or position affording a specific view or vantage; circumstances and programming of an individual that is conducive to a particular response, consideration or belief-set (paradigm); a position (consideration) or place (location) that provides a specific view or perspective (subjective) on experience (of the objective).

postulate : to put forward as truth; to suggest or assume an existence *to be*; to state or affirm the existence of particular conditions; to provide a basis of reasoning and belief; a basic theory accepted as fact; in *Systemology*, Alpha-Thought —the top-most decisions or considerations made by the Alpha-Spirit regarding the "*is-ness*" (what things "are") about energy-matter and space-time.

presence : a quality of some thing (*energy/matter*) being "present" in space-time; personal orientation of *Self* as an *Awareness* (*POV*) located in present space-time (environment) and communicating with extant energy-matter.

processing command line (PCL) : a directed input; a specific command using highly selective language for *Systemology Processing*; a predetermined directive statement (cause) intended to focus concentrated attention (effect).

processing, systematic : the inner-workings or "through-put" result of systems; in *Systemology*, a method of applied spiritual technology used toward personal Self-Actualization; methods of selective directed attention, communicated language and associative imagery that increases personal control of the human condition.

realization : the clear perception of an understanding; a consideration or understanding on what is "actual"; to make "real" or give "reality" to so as to grant a property of "beingness" or "being as it is"; the state or instance of coming to an *Awareness*; in *Systemology*, "gnosis" or true knowledge achieved during *systematic processing*; achievement of a new (or higher) cognition, true knowledge or perception of Self; a consideration of reality or assignment of meaning.

responsibility : the *ability* to *respond*; the extent of mobilizing *power* and *understanding* an individual maintains as *Awareness* to enact *change*; the proactive ability to *Self-direct* and make decisions independent of an outside authority.

Seeker : an individual on the *Pathway to Self-Honesty*; a practitioner of *Mardukite Systemology* or *Systemology Processing*, that is working toward *Spiritual Ascension*.

Self-actualization : bringing the full potential of the Human spirit into Reality; expressing full capabilities and creativeness of the *Alpha-Spirit*.

Self-determinism : the freedom to act, clear of external control or influence; the personal control of Will to direct intention.

Self-honesty : the basic or original *alpha* state of *being* and *knowing*; clear and present total *Awareness* of-and-as *Self*, in its most basic and true proactive expression of itself as *Spirit* or *I-AM*—free of artificial attachments, perceptive filters and other emotionally-reactive or mentally-conditioned programming imposed on the human condition by the systematized physical world; the ability to experience existence without judgment.

spiritual timeline : a continuous stream of moment-to-moment *Mental Images* (or a record of experiences) that defines the "past" of a spiritual being (or *Alpha-Spirit*) and which includes impressions (*imprints, &tc.*) from all life-incarnations and significant spiritual events the being has encountered; in Systemology, also "*backtrack.*"

Spheres of Existence : a series of *eight* concentric circles, rings or spheres (each larger than the former) that is overlaid onto the Standard Model of Beta-Existence to demonstrate the dynamic systems of existence extending out from the POV of Self (often as a "body") at the *First Sphere*; these are given in the basic eightfold systems as: *Self, Home/Family, Groups, Humanity, Life on Earth, Physical Universe, Spiritual Universe* and *Infinity-Divinity*.

Systemology : a modern tradition of applied religious philosophy and spiritual technology based on *Arcane Tablets* (in combination with *"general systemology"* and *"games theory"*) developed in the New Age underground by Joshua Free in 2011 as an advanced futurist extension of the *Mardukite Research Org.*

terminal (node) : a point, end, or mass, on a line; a connection point for closing an electric circuit, such as a post on a battery terminating at each end of its own systematic function; a point of connectivity with other points; in systems, a contact point of interaction; a point of interaction with other points.

turbulence : a quality or state of distortion or disturbance that creates irregularity of a flow or pattern; the quality or state of aberration on a line (such as ragged edges) or the emotional "turbulent feelings" attached to a particular flow or terminal node; a violent, haphazard or disharmonious commotion (such as in the ebb of gusts and lulls of wind action).

validation : a reinforcement of agreements or considerations as being "real."

viewpoint : see *"point-of-view" (POV)*.

willingness : the state of conscious Self-determined ability and interest (directed attention) to *Be, Do* or *Have*; a Self-determined consideration to reach, face up to (*confront*) or manage some "mass" or energy; the extent to which an individual considers themselves able to participate, act or communicate along some line, to put attention or intention on the line, or to produce (create) an effect.

ZU : the ancient Sumerian cuneiform sign for the archaic verb—*"to know," "knowingness"* or *"awareness"*; in *Mardukite Zuism and Systemology*, the active energy/matter of the "Spiritual Universe" (AN) experienced as a *Lifeforce* or *consciousness* that imbues living forms extant in the "Physical Universe" (KI); *"Spiritual Life Energy"*; energy demonstrated by the WILL of an actualized *Alpha-Spirit* in the "Spiritual Universe" (AN), which impinges its *Awareness* into the Physical Universe (KI), animating/controlling *Life* for its experience of *beta-existence* along an individual Alpha-Spirit's personal *Identity-continuum*, called a *ZU-line*.

Zu-Line : a theoretical construct in *Mardukite Zuism and Systemology* demonstrating *Spiritual*

Life Energy (ZU) as a personal individual "continuum" of Awareness interacting with all Spheres of Existence on the Standard Model of Systemology; a spectrum of potential variations and interactions of a monistic continuum or singular *Spiritual Life Energy* demonstrated on the Standard Model; an energetic channel of potential POV and "locations" of Beingness, demonstrated in early Systemology materials as an individual Alpha-Spirit's personal *Identity- continuum*, potentially connecting *Awareness* of *Self* with "*Infinity*" simultaneous with all points considered in existence; a symbolic demonstration of the "*Life-line*" on which *Awareness (ZU)* extends from the direction of the "Spiritual Universe" (AN) in its true original *alpha state* through an entire possible range of activity resulting in its *beta state* and control of a *genetic-entity* occupying the *Physical Universe (KI)*.

Zu-Vision : the true and basic (*Alpha*) Point-of-View (perspective, POV) maintained by *Self* as *Alpha-Spirit* outside boundaries or considerations of the *Human Condition* and *exterior* to beta-existence reality agreements with the Physical Universe; a POV of Self *as* "a unit of Spiritual Awareness" that exists independent of a "body" and entrapment in a *Human Condition*; "spirit vision" in its truest sense.

explore the
Fundamentals of Systemology

All *six*
Basic Course
lesson booklets
in one
hardcover
edition!

start your journey on the
The Pathway to Ascension

All *sixteen*
Professional Course
lesson booklets
in two
hardcover
volumes!

THE SYSTEMOL

Seekers and students of the *Basic Course* and *Professional Course* will also be interested in the *Systemology Core Research Series*. These eight volumes are a complete chronological record of the Mardukite New Thought developments from the Systemology Society, published in 2019 through 2023.

The *Systemology Core* begins with the first professional publication released when the *Mardukite Systemology Society* emerged from the underground in 2019, with: *"The Tablets of Destiny Revelation."*

OGY PATHWAY

PUBLISHED BY THE **JOSHUA FREE** IMPRINT REPRESENTING

The Mardukite Academy of Systemology

mardukite.com

www.ingramcontent.com/pod-product-compliance
Lightning Source LLC
Chambersburg PA
CBHW051002140626
46546CB00017B/2455